W9-AYR-673

J   457517
155.4   14.95
Pat
Patent
Babies!

DATE DUE			

GREAT RIVER REGIONAL LIBRARY

St. Cloud, Minnesota   56301

BABIES!

Dorothy Hinshaw Patent

Holiday House / New York

3611555

To all the family babies, including SEAN

ACKNOWLEDGMENTS

The author wishes to thank Avon Nelson for the idea for this book, Barbara Baird for passing it on, and Margery Cuyler for helping make it what it is. Thanks are also due to David, Jason, Britt, Judy, Laura, Robin, Bonnie, Michael, Lisa, Blacky, Luke, Rebekah, Nichole, Sophie, Peter, Rachel, Alexander, Chelsea, and Sean for giving the author plenty of experience.

The prints and photographs in this book are from the following sources and are used with permission: Title page and pages 3, 7, 12, 15, 20, 25, 27, 29, 33, 39, and 40; Suzanne Szasz. Pages 4, 9, 13; Bruce McMillan. Pages 5 and 37; Sarah Lewis. Page 8; William Muñoz. Pages 10 and 31; Dorothy Hinshaw Patent. Pages 17 and 23; Linda Brooks. Pages 11, 19, and 22; Kathleen M. Kelly. Page 21; West Light. Pages 30, 32, 35, and 36; Georgiana Silk.

Copyright © 1988 by Dorothy Hinshaw Patent
All rights reserved
Printed in the United States of America
First Edition

Library of Congress Cataloging-in-Publication Data

Patent, Dorothy Hinshaw.
Babies!

SUMMARY: Describes the physical, mental, and social development that babies achieve in their first two years of life.
1. Infants—Development—Juvenile literature.
[1. Babies.   2. Child development]   I. Title
RJ134.P38   1988   155.4   87-26663
ISBN 0-8234-0685-7
ISBN 0-8234-0701-2 (pbk.)

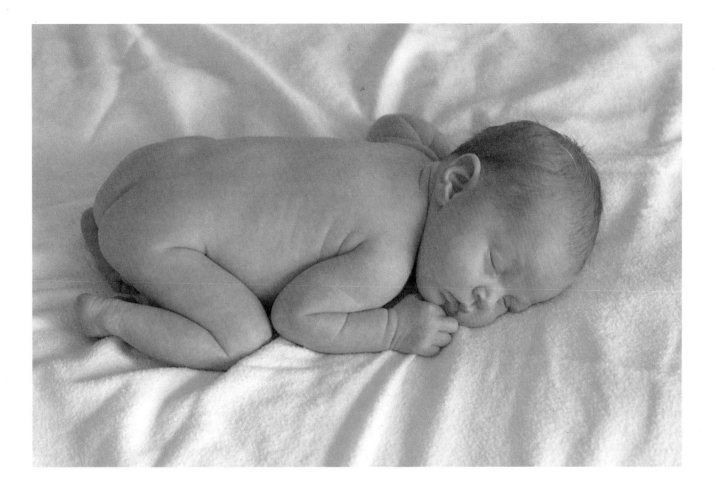

When a baby is born, it goes through the biggest change of its life. Inside the womb, the baby floated in a warm, dark, watery place. The temperature was always about the same. Sounds and movements from the outside were cushioned by the fluid and by the mother's body.

At birth, the baby is thrust into the outside world. For the first time, it feels cool, dry air on its skin. Light hits its eyes, and gravity pulls on its body. It must breathe for itself, and it must cry to show that it is hungry.

457617

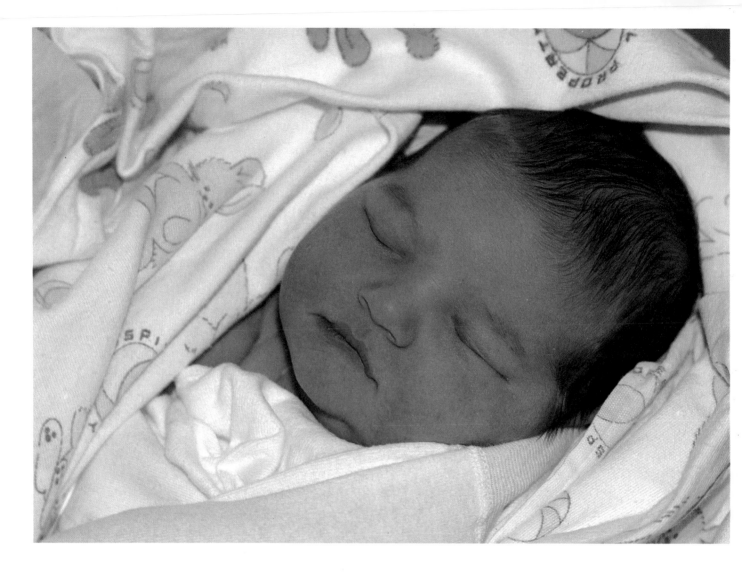

Have you ever seen a newborn baby? The head is very big and is topped with fine hair. The body may be covered with fine, dark fuzz that goes away later. Often the face looks flat or the back of the head looks too long. This is because the baby had to pass through the narrow birth canal. Soon, the soft bones in the head will go back to their normal shape.

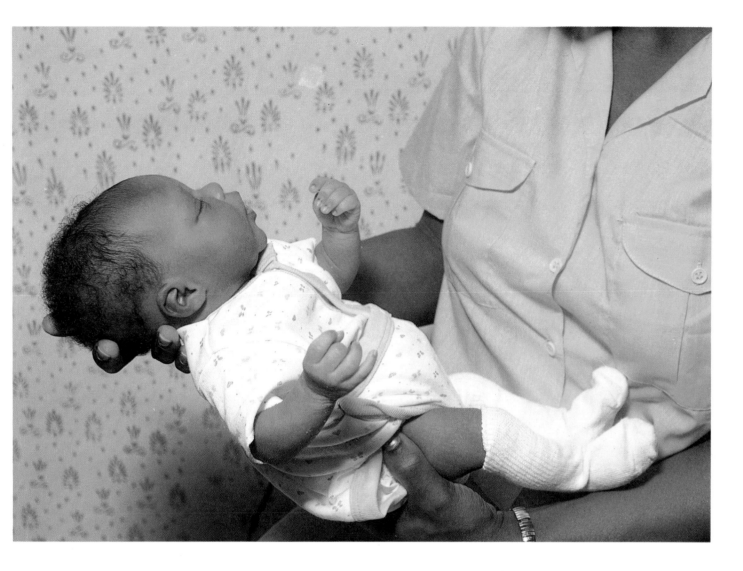

At first the baby can't lift its heavy head. When people carry a new baby, they must be careful to support it. Otherwise, the head will fall backward or to one side. By the time it's three weeks old, a baby can usually hold its head up for a few seconds.

The newborn doesn't have any teeth. For weeks or months, it will feed only on its mother's breast milk or formula from a bottle. Its tongue is designed for sucking. The baby can wrap it around a nipple and pull the milk out easily.

Inside the mother's body, the baby was curled up into a ball. Its legs were bent, and its feet turned inward. These curved legs look strange on a newborn, but they will get straighter in a few weeks.

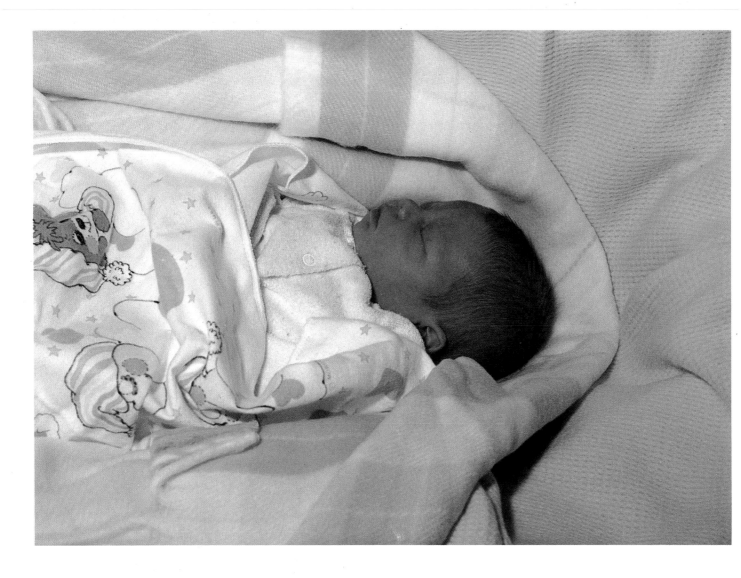

The top of the newborn baby's head is soft. There is a gap between the bones. The baby's brain needs room to get bigger. By the time it is finished growing, the brain will be four times as big as it was when the baby was born.

A newborn baby sleeps most of the time, as much as twenty hours a day. It cries for help when it is hungry, when its diaper is wet or dirty, or when it is in pain.

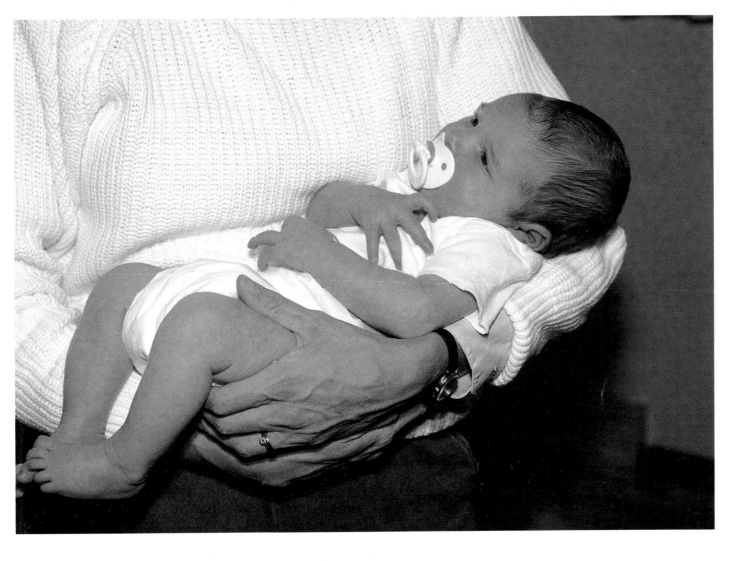

Although the newborn doesn't seem to do much, it is already learning about the world. Touch is its most important sense. The baby is calmed by being held or stroked. By the time it is six weeks old, it can tell the difference between the touch of its mother and its father. It knows if its brother or a stranger has picked it up.

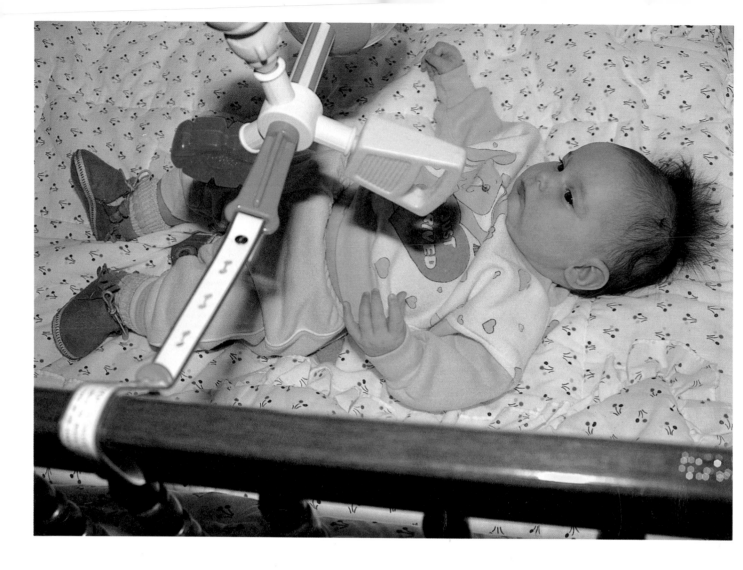

A very young baby may try to look at you, but its eyes can't focus yet. Sometimes, the eyes look crossed. If you want to show a newborn something, hold it about eight inches from the baby's face. That is where its eyes can see best. Young babies are more interested in looking at patterns than in seeing solid colors. They also like to look at human faces.

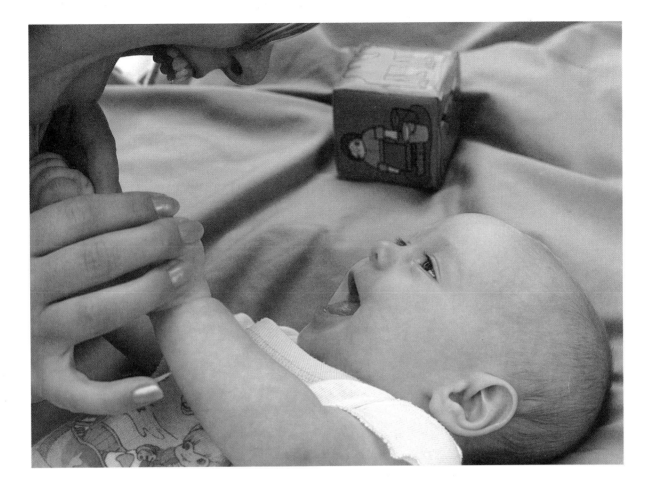

A new baby may smile while it is half asleep and you stroke it gently or hum to it. But it isn't ready to smile yet while awake. That doesn't happen until the baby is three to eight weeks old. Almost all babies are good smilers by four months of age.

No two babies are alike. One may smile three weeks ahead of another baby of the same age. Each newborn is different and develops at its own rate.

The smile is only one way the baby communicates with other people. If you have a new baby in the family, you can learn what it is trying to say if you watch and listen closely.

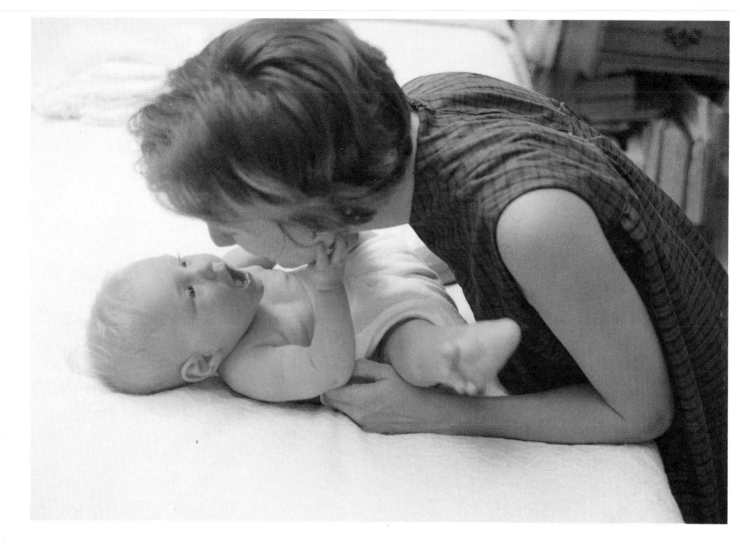

Tiny babies like to be talked to. If you speak gently to
an alert young baby, you may see it make small movements in rhythm with your words. The baby is "talking" back to you with its body.

Babies sometimes want to be left alone. If you are
talking to a baby or showing it things and it keeps
looking away, chances are it is tired of being social.
Give the baby a rest and play with it again later.

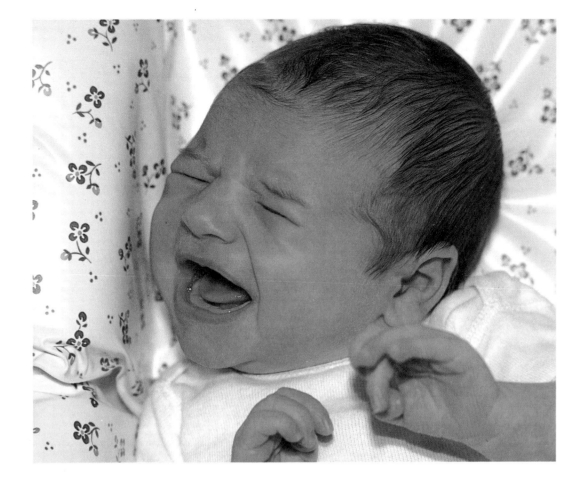

If you listen closely when a baby cries, you may learn to tell what is wrong. A hungry baby repeats the same crying sound over and over, while an angry cry is loud and long. A baby in pain is likely to let out a sudden long cry, then hold its breath. Some babies suffer from colic, loud screaming crying that can't be comforted. They probably have stomachaches. Luckily, colic usually ends by the time a baby is three months old.

Babies also get hiccups after feeding. It may alarm you when the tiny body jerks with a hiccup, but it doesn't bother the baby.

During its first weeks of life, the baby changes very fast. Each day it seems a bit different to those who know it well. It loses its red-faced newborn look, and its legs become straighter. It gets stronger and can usually hold up its head by the end of two months. It smiles more and more often, and before you know it, the baby is "talking."

Long before a baby can speak words, it begins to make sounds other than crying. At four weeks of age, most babies are already making gurgling sounds. During the next few months, the baby experiments with its voice. If you make a sound, the baby may try to imitate it. One baby may "talk" to itself when it is alone in its crib. Another may be quiet when alone but enjoy making baby talk with other people.

The baby is also getting better control of its eyes. By the time most infants are two months old, they can keep their eyes on something interesting and can hold their heads still. This makes it easier for them to see what they are looking at.

By then, the baby knows the difference between a family member and a stranger. It may smile at someone it doesn't know but look serious at the sight of a sister wearing sunglasses or with a new hairdo. The baby recognizes the face, but knows that something is different about it.

As a baby gets older, it spends more time awake. And when it sleeps, it stays asleep longer. It needs to feed less often, too. Bit by bit, the baby gets into a regular schedule of sleeping, eating, and being awake.

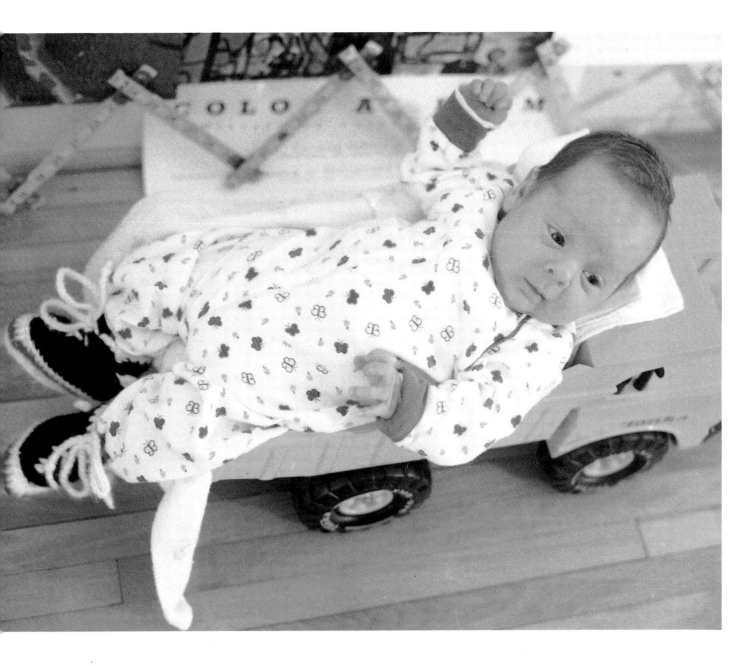

At first, a baby's hands are almost always closed loosely into tiny fists. If you put a rattle in its hand, the baby will hold it tight. The rattle will make lots of noise because of the jerky movements of the baby's arm. But by its second month, a baby usually starts to control its hands. You might see it bat at an object such as a mobile hanging over its crib. Those early swings of the arm are jerky, but they are the beginnings of an exciting new stage in the baby's life. Soon it will be able to pick up things by itself.

Grasping an object takes time to learn. The eyes must judge where it is, and the hand must move just that far. The hand has to be open at the right time and close just enough to pick up the object without dropping it or crushing it. It takes a baby a long time to learn this task.

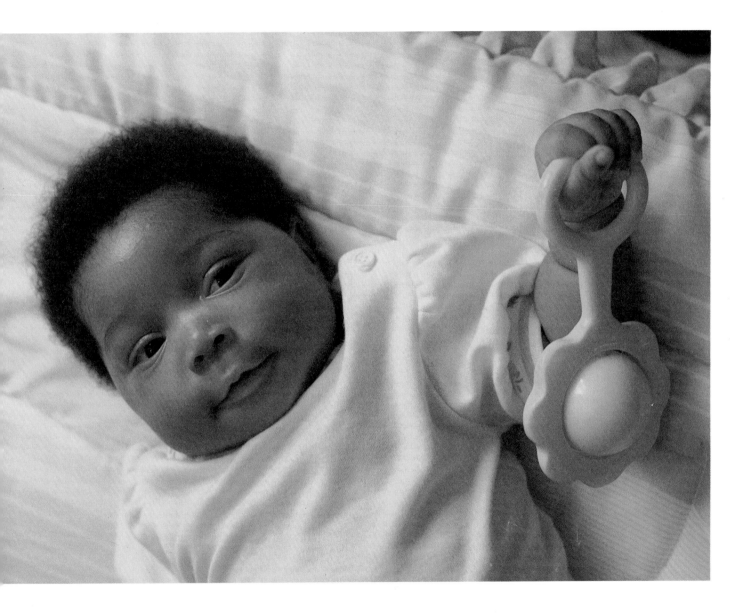

About the same time the baby can grab and hold things, it becomes fascinated with its hands. It plays with its fingers, bringing them together, spreading them out, and grabbing one hand with the other. It can also jam its fist into its mouth. A baby's mouth is very sensitive, and the infant uses it to explore objects. Anything you put into its hand is likely to end up in its mouth. It is important never to give a baby something to hold which it shouldn't put into its mouth.

Most babies really enjoy their baths by now. They smile and splash their arms and legs in excitement. Some young babies have a scaly patch on their heads called cradle cap. It looks strange, but it doesn't harm the baby. If the head is carefully washed every bath time, the cradle cap will go away.

At three months, a baby has become a giving family member. Its smiles and sounds bring joy to others. Most babies sleep through the night by then, so their families can get a good rest. Many babies start eating cereal now, the first step in varying their diet. Life begins to settle down to normal, and it is hard to imagine not having that new person in the family.

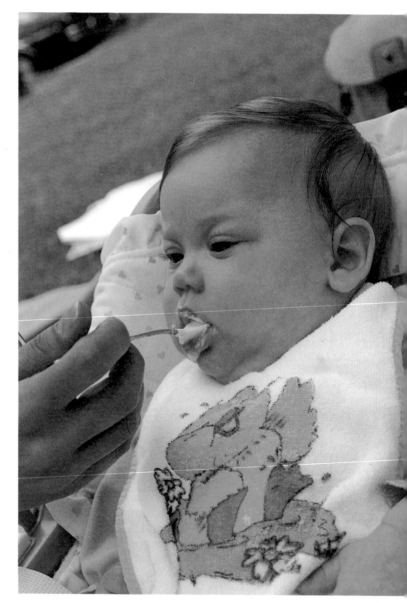

Getting stronger is very important for the baby. It spends a lot of time putting its weight on its arms, then hands, when lying on its tummy. It also starts pulling its legs under its body so that its bottom is up in the air. All this effort pays off. By three months, it can sit up with support and at four months, it can roll from its stomach or side to its back.

When you hold the baby now, it will treat you like a living jungle gym! It will bounce up and down, bending and straightening its knees, if you stand it on your lap.

As the baby gets older, it needs to be with other people as much as possible. Babies like to be where the action is. Just watching Mother fix dinner or keeping Brother and Sister company while they play can be fun for the baby. Its eyes keep getting better until, by four months, it can see as well as an adult. It enjoys seeing bright colors and looking out the window while riding in the car. These activities are a lot more interesting than lying alone in a crib.

There are plenty of games you can play with a baby to make it smile and later, laugh. Peekaboo and pat-a-cake are always favorites. You can invent your own little games, too, that just you and the baby can enjoy together.

Around six months, the baby gets its first tooth, usually one of the bottom ones in the front of the mouth. In a month or so, that tooth is joined by its mate on the other side. Now when the baby smiles, it has two shiny teeth. From this time on, new teeth come in regularly. Soon after the bottom front teeth appear, the top two arrive. Until age two, more and more teeth emerge. Often when a new tooth is coming in, the baby will drool. It may also pull on its jaws or ears. Itching gums can make the baby fretful, and some babies appreciate having the gums gently rubbed to help ease the itching.

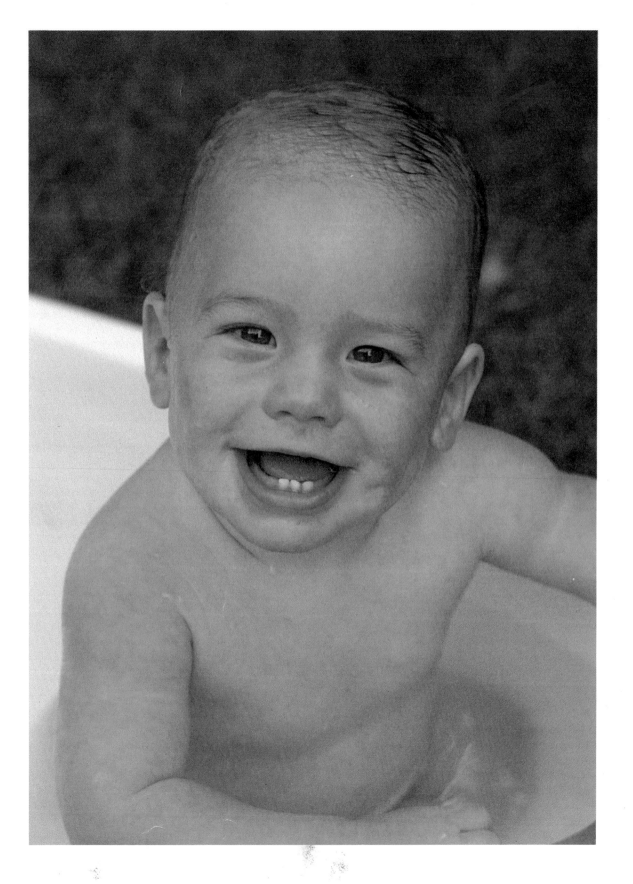

The six-month-baby is lots of fun to have around. By then, most babies give as much as they get while playing with their families. They may wave at you or call out to catch your attention so you'll play. They can control many body movements and can pick things up with their hands. Many six-month-old babies have discovered their feet and may even enjoy sucking on their toes.

Six months is a turning point for the baby. Until then, it couldn't do much for itself. But during the next few weeks, the baby will figure out how to roll completely over, and it will begin to creep along on its stomach. Before, you could set the baby down on a bed without worry. Now it might roll off and get hurt. Once you could put the baby in the middle of the floor with a few toys and leave the room. Now you have to be sure nothing dangerous can be reached from anywhere on the floor.

Usually by eight or nine months, a baby can sit up all by itself. Now a whole new world of play opens up. It can reach out and grab different toys. If put on the floor with a choice of playthings, the baby can enjoy itself while the rest of the family works or plays nearby.

By the time a baby can sit up well, it is usually able to crawl from place to place, too. Crawling adds wonderful freedom for the baby, but a crawling baby can get into trouble very quickly. It can spot an electric cord across the room. In a flash, the cord is in the baby's mouth. Crawling goes with curiosity, but not with any common sense.

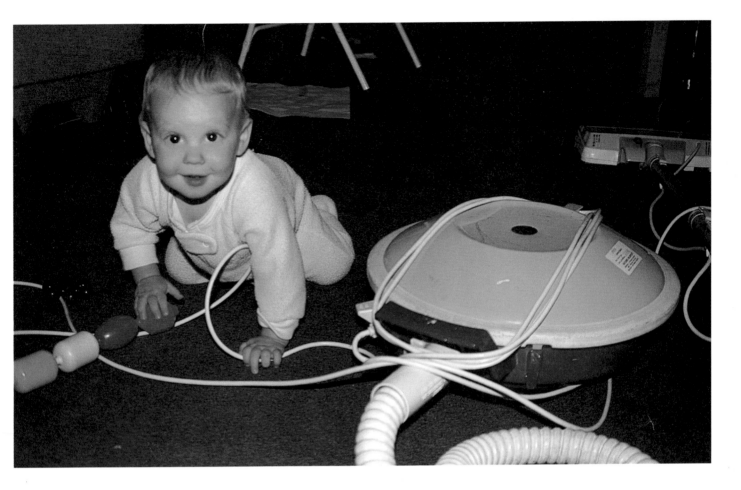

Between six months and a year, the baby gets more demanding about what it wants. It can become fascinated by a full wastebasket. No matter how many times you tell it no and move the wastebasket away, it will keep crawling back. The baby's voice is also louder and when it wants something, it lets everyone know.

Babies this age become very attached to their mothers. They get upset whenever Mother leaves the room. No one else, even a brother or sister, can ease the pain. This stage can be difficult for everyone. Mother can't always be with the baby, and other family members may feel hurt that they can't provide comfort.

Most babies can stand by the end of their first year. They learn by holding onto the furniture or the bars of their cribs. The problem is, the baby usually can't figure out how to get back down. It will pull itself up, hand over hand along the leg of a table, and stand for a few moments. Then it will cry miserably because it is stuck upright. Luckily, this stage doesn't last too long. Within a couple of weeks, most babies figure out either how to plop on their bottoms or how to work their hands back down the support as they lower themselves to the floor.

As the baby gets closer to its first birthday, it will like to look at books. You can turn pages for the baby, pointing out objects. Soon, when you ask "Where is the kitty?", the baby can point to the cat itself. You can show the baby how to put blocks in a box, and it will try to copy you.

By the time the baby is a year old, it needs lots of toys for entertainment. It wants to explore anything and everything, and its own rattles and beads get boring very fast. It will enjoy playing with pots and pans on the kitchen floor and shaking car keys. Toys small enough for a baby to swallow, toys with sharp edges, and stuffed animals with eyes that can be pulled off are not safe.

During its first year, a baby does a lot of growing up. By one year of age, most babies can sit, crawl, and babble so well that it sounds like real talking. Some babies have words, too, often ones they have made up but that the family can understand. The one-year-old can understand much of what you say. It may wave "bye-bye" if asked, and might bring you a toy when requested. Some one-year-olds can even walk a few, halting steps. But to cross the open spaces, they drop down to the floor and crawl. At this stage, many babies enjoy walking while holding firmly onto the hands of an older member of the family.

The exciting moment comes when the baby walks with both hands free. Baby's first step is a big moment for everyone in the family. It is usually followed with a plop down onto the floor. But before long, the baby will be toddling across the room. Babies at this stage are called "toddlers" because of their special way of walking. Their feet don't have arches yet, and with each step, the whole foot lands at once. They have trouble keeping their balance, yet after a few weeks, they rarely fall down. Once the baby can walk alone, it has real freedom to explore the world on its own.

Learning to talk is exciting both for the baby and for other members of the family. Around a year, most babies know two or three words, usually the names of family members or pets. Bit by bit for the next few months, new words are added. It seems as if the baby will never learn enough words to really communicate. Then, at about eighteen months, many words suddenly appear. Every day there is something new, and everyone is excited. Soon after, the baby starts combining two words together to get messages across—"naughty dog," "want cookie," "go park," and so forth. The youngest member of the family is now well on the way to knowing how to express things to others.

But learning to talk is individual. Many very bright children barely talk before they are two years old, some even later. We really understand little about how speech develops. Each family needs to be patient and accept the pace set by its own toddler.

As the baby heads towards its second birthday, it wants to know about everything. Drawers need to be opened, windows have to be peered through. One of the first phrases many babies learn is "What's zat?" They point to everything in sight and ask the same question. This is both fun and difficult for other family members, who always tire of the game before the baby does. But by being so curious about the world and so eager to learn, babies find out new things all the time. That curiosity is what helps the infant make the gradual change from being a baby to being a child.